ST. MARY'S COLLEGE OF EDUCATION

DATE BORROWED

BOOKS TO BE RETURNED ONE WEEK FROM DATE

26. APR. 1971

D1436395

THE BROKEN PLACES

THE BROKEN PLACES

poems by

GEORGE MACBETH

SCORPION PRESS

First published in March 1963 by
Scorpion Press
Manor House, Pakefield Street, Lowestoft, Suffolk

© *1963 George MacBeth*
Reprinted 1965

Printed by Villiers Publications Ltd.,
Ingestre Road, London, N.W.5

This book is dedicated to
2nd Lt. George MacBeth
killed through enemy action
October 20th 1941
and to
Amelia Morton Mary MacBeth
Died in hospital
April 20th 1951

' If people bring so much courage to this world the world has to break them, so of course it kills them. The world breaks every one and afterward many are strong at the broken places. But those that will not break it kills. It kills the very good and the very gentle and the very brave impartially. If you are none of these you can be sure it will kill you too but there will be no special hurry. . . .'

Ernest Hemingway: A Farewell To Arms

Some of these poems have appeared, or will shortly appear, in the following magazines and anthologies: *Best Poems of 1960 (U.S.A.)*, *The Carleton Miscellany (U.S.A.)*, *The Critical Quarterly*, *A Group Anthology*, *The Listener*, *The London Magazine*, *Modern Poetry for Schools*, *New Lines*, *New Poems 1960*, *New Poems 1961*, *New Poems 1962*, *New Poems 1963*, *The New Poets of England and America (U.S.A.)*, *The New Statesman*, *The New Yorker (U.S.A.)*, *The Observer*, *The Paris Review (U.S.A.)*, *The Secondary Modern Anthology*, *The Times Literary Supplement*, *The Transatlantic Review (U.S.A.)*, *The Twentieth Century*, *Words in Place;* some have been broadcast in *The Living Poet* and *New Poetry* on the B.B.C. Third Programme and in *About the House* and *Poets and Poetry* on the B.B.C. Home Service; and some have appeared in a Fantasy Press pamphlet, *Lecture to the Trainees;* to the editors of these magazines, anthologies and radio programmes, and to the Fantasy Press, my acknowledgements are due.

CONTENTS

I

EARLY WARNING

Lord god of wings, forgive this hand
That stole from thee. These holy bones
Where thy long shadow ran I give
Thee back, repentant. From thy dead
Steel bird's ripped belly I and four
Doomed ice-men took them out, eight hands

Fouling thy sacred felled limbs. Two
Dropped bones I stooped and kicked. Forgive
Me, god. I never knew thy bones,
Delivered from the ice, could rise
And kill four men. I thought thou wast
Mortal as I. Thy lofty skull,

Smoothed by the Greenland wind, I stole
With my scarred hands. I thought last night
That whale-fat poured in thy round eyes
Would staunch the wind. If my hut stands
And others fell, no other cause
I seek for that. So when at dawn

Four ice-men died, burnt-up by thy
Bones' wrath, I thought : this jealous god's
Enduring skull, strong thigh-bone, I
Must give back safe, wise helps, sure harms
For cruel men. Forgive me, god,
For what I did. Those men thou burned

With inward hell that made them twist
In wrangling heaps were faithless. I
Repent my sin. If I should carve
A cross for thee, draped with a fish
Nailed through its hanging tail, wouldst thou
Dismiss this pain? I feel it come

Below the eyes, inside my head,
As they all said it came. Forgive
My theft. I give thee back thy skull,
Thy scalding thigh-bone, god. Thou shalt
Own all I have, my hut, my wife,
My friendly pack of dogs, if thou

Wilt only tell why these green scars
Ache in my cheeks; why this grey mould
Forms on my herring pail; why this
Right hand that touched thy head shrinks up;
And why this living fish I touched
Writhes on that plank, spoiled food for gulls?

ASH

So it was true. Elastic air could fill
    In a trice with particles
   And clapped earth give no warning. Ill
    With rage, they swallowed pills,
Floundered to hide-outs. Over the hogback Southern hills

A giant sifter shook black sugar. Bleeps
    On the tele-screen spelled SLEEP
   IT THROUGH. Eyes glued on sky-fed slag-heaps
    Peppering soot, watched sheep
Whose wool stank acrid stick at stiles no legs could leap.

The crushed air gently settled. In a slow
    Powdering like a crow's
   Wing mouldering, a thin tar snow
    Assembled, staining toes
Of barefoot children dug in sand it cast no shadows

In but mingled with. What fitter night
    For prophesying flights
   Of rooks? In entrails needles might
    Probe omens. Grilled in tights,
A Creole whore screamed giving birth. Her brat's paired
        whites

Shone like burnt coals. A negro steeplejack
    Nine floors up welding cracks
   In scaffolding shrivelled on a rack
    Of poisoned iron. Packs
Of wolves burned. Chessboard queens in stained teak spat like
        sacks

Of roasted chestnuts on a grated fire
Of sulphur. A Church choir's
Top alto charred. His Chrysler tyre
Made licorice. The spire's
Incinerating copper boiled a bat. *Esquires*

Where clutching fingers curled, shrank into what
Crumbled like bad flour, blots
Of putrefying matter, hot
As frying kidneys. Shots
Of iced Scotch would have cooled one soldier's nerve-ends.
Dots

And dashes flustered angry dials. Done
Steaks grilled. Not everyone's
Plop-footed warden, won
From melting wax, brought guns
To fortify stuffed cellars. When one came, few suns,

Rotting the bricked fumes, twisted through taut sashes
To explore a livid gash
Of wounded air where crackling lashes
Writhed. More times that rash
Of acid yellow faltered. What was left was ash.

MOTHER SUPERIOR

Sisters, it will be necessary
To prepare a cool retreat. See to
It that several basins are filled
Nightly with fresh water and placed there.
Take care that food for a long stay be

Provided in sealed jars. I know of
No way to protect an outer room
From the light but some must be tried. Let
The walls be made thick to keep out the
Heat. Before the Annunciation

Our Lord exacts no other service.
It may seem prudent to wear a wool
Robe at all times and to bow down when
The Word comes. Remember the parable
Of the Virgins and pray for all the

Unpremeditating. ' The brides of
Our Lord in their burrows ' may not be
A flattering title but the known
Future lies in the wombs of prepared
Rabbits. To bear a pure strain with no

Care for the world's corruption requires
Courage, sisters. Creating a safe
Place for the incarnation of what
One can scarcely imagine without
Madness might seem a demeaning task.

In the Order of Resurrection
Of which you are acolytes there is
No more noble service. Remember
The Code. Your duty is not to the
Sick but to the unborn. Perform it.

THE SON

Her body was all stones. She lay
In the stones like a glass marble. There was
      No moisture in her. There
Was only the dry spleen and the liver
    Gone hard as pumice-stone. I closed

Her eyes. I saw a sole once on
A block of green marble. It was flung straight
      From the living brine, its
Pupils were bright with a strange heat. I watched
    A cat eat it alive. When I

Touched her cheek, the light failed. When I
Moved my open hand on her lips, there was
      No life there. She smelled of
The cheap soap we had washed her in. I saw
    The black hollows below her eyes

Where desire swam. I called her name
In the dark, but no-one answered. There was
      Only the sap rising.
I thought of the clotted mercury in
    The broken thermometer of

Her body. It rose again in
My head to a silver column, a sword
      Of blood in the sun. I
Held to its cross of fire in a dream of
    Climbing. I swam in the air : my

Wings were extended into the
Night. I was borne above the clouds : I flew
      At increasing speeds, to
Increasing altitudes. There was only
    The sun above me. I *was* the

Sun. The world was my mother, I
Spread my wings to protect her growth. She broke
    Into wheat and apples
Beneath my rain. I came with my fire to
    The sea, to the earth from the air,

    To the broken ground with my fresh
Seed. I lay on her cold breast, inhaling
    The scent of iris and
Daffodils. There was nothing more to be
    Settled. I thought of her dying

    Words, how butter would scarcely melt
In her mouth. I heard a wheel squeak and the
    Drip of water. I touched
The cold rail and the covering sheet. Your
    Light shone in my eyes. Forgive me.

A CONFESSION

Was it alive? I often asked myself
And avoided the answer. I called it something cooking,
Curled up and rising, soft shapeless matter
Stuck to my greased sides waiting to be born.
But once or twice in the small hours I lay thinking
That it could feel things : it was warm in its wet cave,
Swimming and feeding like a baby shrimp there;
And then the hard cold inrush of its killer,
Saw-teeth, threshing fins, cascading water,
And the soul spat like a bubble out of its head,
Three months old. I don't know when they're shaped
Like things you can see are children. I was afraid
To look the books up. I've imagined monsters
At three months : or at best like pancake men,
Things from a dream, radiation monsters.
Under the anaesthetic I dreamed nothing.
But one night for the pain they gave me morphia.
I had a strange dream then, worse than a nightmare.
I was in the baby : do you follow me? *in* it.
I'd felt them pull it out : then it grew huge,
Filled the small ward, it was throbbing bloody matter
Soft inside like a cooling hot-cross bun,
And I was in the middle, six blobs of dough
Not feeling anything. Then I woke up
Sweating with pain : no baby, nothing but darkness
Ticking with clocks, dripping with water, and blood
From clots of cotton-wool sopping through my night-dress.
It was me in pain : and I'd thought my baby was
That never lived perhaps to feel a pain.
O God those rubber gloves! It makes me squirm
To think of all that fingering to feel it!
White legs in waders floundering among eels!
After the rabbit-tests they weren't quite sure
So it was stage two : get in there and look.
Those enemas! You've just got no idea
What soap pumped up your bottom when you're twenty
Feels like : as if you're six with constipation.

I could have blushed all over. Then it was jabs
To make me dozy, so I stayed awake,
Partly to hear the anaesthetist make jokes
In the theatre, like when I had tonsils out
And wouldn't nod off, partly out of fear,
And partly simply wanting to be *there*
At something vital to me : in at the death.
I wasn't, though. Their faces flooded out
And I came back above my emptied body
On a steel trolley in the ante-room,
Detached, cool, with voices discussing me.
I felt relaxed, free, till the pain began.
It wasn't bad at first : just aching rubbing
From an internal graze : but it was agony
Like ripping bandages from the middle of my guts
When the plugs came out. It became routine.
Each morning, screens : and forceps picking at me,
Dismembering the corpse in penny numbers.
That last day was the worst. Like having the curse
Worse than when it's worst. I was having a baby
Born in bits. I could recognise it then :
Solid : not blood : I could see cells and things.
For two months since I've kept on wondering
Did it all come out? They said I'd take
A while to adjust to it, but I know for sure
It might be growing again from one bit left,
A resurrected monster, like a giant lizard
Sprung from a tadpole, gathering itself for revenge
On me and its father. What makes it terrifying is
I'd never seen him before. Even his Christian name
Slithers away when I try to think. That sofa
Wedged by the wall, and gawping at television
(The Perry Como Show) I remember that
And that's about all. Before I'd felt it coming
As more than motion, rapid, clumsy, not pleasant
Up-and-down jerking, it was over. This last half-hour
I've started noticing the Virgin Mary
Above the altar. Suppose she'd not believed
She was to be Christ's mother, taken precautions,

Aborted Him. Would anyone have blamed her
For not being taken in by wishful visions?
She was, though. She believed what she was told
And the child was born that God was Father to,
Planted by the angel. Listen, now : suppose
I was the victim of an angel, too,
One with powerful fins and the ability to live
Between these pink doors for days without weakening
Or dropping his wand. Only two people would know
If Christ came back I might have murdered Him
And you'd be one of them. You've said on Sundays
We're punished for our sins. What could mine be
For crucifying someone in my womb?

THE GOD OF LOVE

'The musk-ox is accustomed to near-Arctic conditions. When danger threatens, these beasts cluster together to form a defensive wall or a "porcupine" with the calves in the middle.'

Dr. Wolfgang Engelhardt : ' Survival of The Free '.

I found them between far hills, by a frozen lake,
    On a patch of bare ground. They were grouped
  In a solid ring, like an ark of horn. And around
    Them circled, slowly closing in,
Their tongues lolling, their ears flattened against the wind,

  A whirlpool of wolves. As I breathed, one fragment of bone
      and
    Muscle detached itself from the mass and
  Plunged. The pad of the pack slackened, as if
    A brooch had been loosened. But when the bull
Returned to the herd, the revolving collar was tighter. And
      only

  The windward owl, uplifted on white wings
    In the glass of air, alert for her young,
  Soared high enough to look into the cleared centre
    And grasp the cause. To the slow brain
Of each beast by the frozen lake what lay in the cradle of their
      crowned

  Heads of horn was a sort of god-head. Its brows
    Nudged when the ark was formed. Its need
  Was a delicate womb away from the iron collar
    Of death, a cave in the ring of horn
Their encircling flesh had backed with fur. That the collar of
      death

Was the bone of their own skulls : that a softer womb
    Would open between far hills in a plunge
Of bunched muscles : and that their immortal calf lay
    Dead on the snow with its horns dug into
The ice for grass : they neither saw nor felt. And yet if

That hill of fur could split and run — like a river
    Of ice in thaw, like a broken grave —
It would crack across the icy crust of withdrawn
    Sustenance and the rigid circle
Of death be shivered : the fed herd would entail its underfur

On the swell of a soft hill and the future be sown
    On grass, I thought. But the herd fell
By the bank of the lake on the plain, and the pack closed,
    And the ice remained. And I saw that the god
In their ark of horn was a god of love, who made them die.

THE KILLING

In a wooden room, surrounded by lights and
    Faces, the place where death had
Come to its sharpest point was exposed. In a
    Clear shell they examined the
    Needle of death. How many
   Million deaths were concentrated in

A single centre ! The compass of death was
    Lifted, detached and broken,
Taken and burned. The seed of death lay in the
    Hold. Without disturbance or
    Ceremony they sealed it
   In foil. The ship stirred at the quay. The

Pilot was ready. A long shadow slanted
    On the harbour water. The
Fin bearing the ignorant crew on their brief
    Journey cut through the air. Three
    Furlongs out at sea the
   Strike of the engine fell. The screws turned

At ease on the rim of the world. The hour had
    Come. The action was taken.
The doors opened. And the ash went out to sea
    Borne with the moon on the tide
    Away from the shore towards the
   Open water. The shell rocked on the

Livid waves. The captain washed his hands in the
    Salt to cleanse the illusion
Of blood. The light casket lay on the soaked planks
    Emptied of all it held. And
    A pale fish that used to leap
   For a fly or a grub to the bare

Trees and then sink back to the living water
    Forgot the way : and died in
The dry branches. The baked island was crusted
    With the blue eggs of terns from
    Which no soft wings would ever
   Break to fly in the sun. And the raw

Turtle crawled inland instead of towards the
    Sea, believing the parched soil
Would change to sand again. They thought the killing
    Was over : but the needle
    Had run wild in the shell. The
   Poison was in the salt current of

The world. Let no Jew or Gentile believe that
    The fly in the brain of the
Bald man adjusting his earphones annuls his
    Own nature; nor pity the
    Man imprisoned for stealing
   Fire from heaven. He, too, is guilty.

REPORT TO THE DIRECTOR

I'd say their marble cubicles were a shade
Too small for the taller men, but they all appeared
To be standing at ease. O the usual postures — hands
In their pockets, hands on their hips, hands on the wall.
A few touched themselves. A few were saying prayers
Perhaps. I expect a few were feeling the cold
From that bare cement floor in those bedroom slippers.
I did, in my shoes; but still, I suppose one allows
A little latitude in the provinces. No money
To do it all in style. However, it worked
And we did get going. One man was reluctant
To co-operate about buttons — a big fellow
With a lot of weight to throw around : it's always
Annoying that sort of thing : a nasty business
It can be on those tiles. So we gave a hand,
Igor and I. The locals didn't mind,
They rarely do. From there it was plain sailing
To the main business. The five attendants came
All according to the book, well-turned-out men
In their new aprons, with the usual hoses, and a good
Flexible pump. (I gave them marks for that. You know
There's a lot of friction on those grids if they scuffle
When you fit the neck-plates.
It might be worthwhile specifying cable,
Steel-strapped stuff; it would save in the long run.)
Fortunately, we didn't need it : they were all so docile,
Queued and shuffled out with no trouble at all.
Though the line-up was tricky — they'd done the count wrong
So we had to use the shoe-horn on a couple.
But after that it was fine : taps on,
Mask fitted, the legs well held, the right grip
And a nice simple injection — I always think
Those gas-cylinders are all wrong. The infusion
Was one of the smoothest I've seen. Evacuation
Very decent. An infinity of freshness
In a little diffusion of bitter carbolic. Rather sweet.
It took about fifteen minutes to get the stories,

And not much mess : they had to scrub the channel
To clear some vomit, otherwise all O.K.
No frills : but at least the operation was completed
With all proper precautions, the doors closed,
The men screened : and, O yes, the windows open
To clean the air. I doubt if anyone smelled
A rat in the whole building, or heard as much
As a squeak from a plimsoll. They moved like professionals
From start to finish. I'd say it was all good work.
They certainly do things with the minimum fuss.
I'd recommend we exonerate the whole depot.

DROP

Sky was the white soil you
Grew in. When the fourth stick broke
      Into thistledown
At the crack of a whistle, streaked brown

    From the crutch out with a crust
Of fear it was like an orgasm to
      Fork into air.
I could see why they'd nicked that nylon

    Rip-cord ' the release '. We
Spread like a leprosy on their clean
      Sun to the wogs. You
Could see their screwed heads grow up

    Like dry coal we'd got
To clap a match to. Christ it was good
      To feel the sick
Flap of the envelope in the wind :

    Like galloping under a stallion's
Belly. Half of Africa flushed
      Out and cocked
Up : you could piss in its eye. You could want to

    Scream the Marseillaise like a
Hymn. And then it was all gone.
      Splum. You were sinking
In a hot bog you'd never wrench

    Clear of alive. Soaked,
Vomiting, jelly-marrowed, afraid
      To spit. No life
Left but that leg-breaking drop on a

Split stockade where they'd have your
Genitals off. You were strung up like Jesus
        Christ in the strings
Of your own carriage : lynched by the Kosher

    Sluts who'd packed your chute.
It couldn't work. You were on your own.
        The stick had died
In the screws or never dropped. When the ground

    Slammed you at eighteen feet
Per second you were out skedaddling for the first
        Tree with your harness
Cut : the sten jammed whore-

    hot yammering out of your
Groin. You were implementing the drill
        Balls : it was flog
On till you blacked out dead.

THE DISCIPLE

I wore a black band. I thought
They would crucify Him in jail. The
Word broke from His agony in the cells. I
Awoke transfigured by incarnate
Will. When He walked out alive I knew
That He was our Saviour. I remember His
Burned face sharp in a nimbus
Of blurred light against the taut flags when He spoke

To our massed lifted hands at
The Rally. I knelt chilled by the bare
Marble before the fed flame for His dead
Martyrs. I knew in my caught heart we
Must all repeat His suffering. I
Wept the oath. I was dedicated to the
Stern commitments of a snapped
Order. I swore to purify my blood of

Evil. I accepted the
Fires of hell on earth. Each uniform
I wore was as my flesh. Its coarse fibres were
Burned by Evil, scraped bare of dust of
Evil, encrusted with excrement
Of Evil. I breathed Evil in the stench of
The bean soup we drank, the bags
Of charcoal I unheaped for the furnaces,

The pit of my soul. When I
Raked the ovens or even touched a
Spade I felt sick. I vomited when I saw
The pyramid of their bodies for
The first time. When a crying child stretched
Out her arms to me I was moved to sweep her
Clear of the doors. I was not
A strong-willed man. I fought to do the hard thing

Well but the Evil within
Me fought back. I lay awake hearing
Them scream. I committed the sin of pity
For Evil every time I touched
Their brittle limbs. In my dreams I was
Watching my infant sister crawled on by stick
Insects with human faces.
Gas was like incense : it drowned corruption. In

The wind or in cylinders
To be raised and used it became a
Presence more real than His. Above my bed
His tense eyes looked down while I slept and
Forgave or condemned. His enormous
Words on the air proved that He still existed
And surely cared : but I held
A scarred ikon close to my heart which showed Him

Massacred in the streets by
The Blood of Evil. I walked in the
Foul heresy of admiring His weakness
More than His rise to power : but I
Groped my way back. The laceration
Of conscience began to ease. And the toil of
Confronting the Evil in
Others began to confront the Evil in

Me. I was helped. I confessed
My doubts. I endured the controlling
Speech and hands of those more sure in their faith than
I. And by Grace I recovered my
Sanity and was purified in
Body and spirit. Behind a locked door in
A blaze of light on a plain
Slate floor my schism was healed by the salt of

Fear. I have no stain left to
Scour. I cut into your wire a saved
Man. I am freed from sin by the mechanism
Of holy justice. I heard of His
Death as if the meaning of Life had
Been for a moment suspended but felt no
Grief. I have shed my heavy
Cross and abide my end in peace of spirit.

THE DREAM

The air kept faith. Between eight
And eleven the angels of Death
Paused. We held each other to the beat of our
　　Own blood. I dreamed of our two bodies
　　Burning on water. The veil of the
Temple was rent and about the ninth hour there
　　　　Was fornication throughout
The kingdom. The fire went from the bones into

　　The blue air. The sentry at
　　The barricade was aware of no
Particle of the myth dying. It was all
　　Rising in a slow spiral. I nursed
　　A sense of returning. I owned these
Flooded corridors like my own grave. I was
　　　　In the attack. We were all
Hurled over the top in a hail of iron

　　Crosses. My booted feet were
　　In mud, my gloved hands were on my head.
I was up to my neck in water. I screamed
　　Once. I began to walk, slithering
　　A little on wet concrete, towards
The white ring of light in the distance. It grew
　　　　As I approached it. The faint
Echo grew in the labyrinth of my ears.

　　The lift burst from the mountain
　　Into the blue air. The eagle was
Circling above the peak. Far off I could hear
　　The music of *Siegfried*. As I stepped
　　From the stone cage to the soft ground I
Could smell her hair against my shoulder. I spat
　　　　My own blood out. The dog ran
Barking across the clean snow. It was over.
　　　　　　　　Fuehrerbunker, April 29th, 1945.

II

THE DRAWER

Their belongings were buried side by side
In a shallow bureau drawer. There was her
Crocodile handbag, letters, a brooch,
All that was in the bedside cupboard
And a small green jar she'd had for flowers.

My father's were in an envelope :
A khaki lanyard, crushed handkerchief,
Twelve cigarettes, a copying-pencil,
All he had on him when he was killed
Or all my mother wanted to keep.

I put them together seven years ago.
Now that we've moved, my wife and I,
To a house of our own, I've taken them out.
Until we can find another spare drawer
They're packed in a cardboard box in the hall.

So this dead, middle-aged, middle-class man
Killed by a misfired shell, and his wife
Dead of cirrhosis, have left one son
Aged nine, aged nineteen, aged twenty-six,
Who has buried them both in a cardboard box.

THE COMPASSES

Baroque-handled and sharp
With blunt lead in their lips
And their fluted legs together
My father's compasses
Lie buried in this flat box.

I take it out of its drawer,
Snap old elastic bands
And rub the frayed leatherette :
It smells faintly of smoke :
The broken hinges yawn.

As I level the case to look
A yellowed protractor claps
Against black-papered board,
Sliding loose in the lid
Behind a torn silk flap.

I look in the base at the dusty
Velvet cavities :
Dead-still, stiff in the joints
And side by side they lie
Like armoured knights on a tomb.

One by one I lift
Them out in the winter air
And wipe some dust away :
Screw back their gaping lips
And bend the rigid knees.

In an inch of hollowed bone
Two cylinders of lead
Slither against each other
With a faint scurrying sound.
I lay them carefully back

And close the case. In Crookes
My father's bones are scattered
In a measured space of ground :
Given his flair for drawing
These compasses should be there

Not locked away in a box
By an uninstructed son
But like an Egyptian king's
Ready shield and swords
Beside his crumbling hand.

THE MINER'S-HELMET

My father wore it working coal at Shotts
When I was one. My mother stirred his broth
And rocked my cradle with her shivering hands
While this black helmet's long-lost miner's-lamp
Showed him the road home. Through miles of coal
His fragile skull, filled even then with pit-props,
Lay in a shell, the brain's blue-printed future
Warm in its womb. From sheaves of saved brown paper,
Baring an oval into weeks of dust,
I pull it down : its laced straps move to admit
My larger brows; like an abdicated king's
Gold crown of thirty years ago, I touch it
With royal fingers, feel its image firm —
Hands grown to kings' hands calloused on the pick,
Feet slow like kings' feet on the throneward gradient
Up to the coal-face — but the image blurs
Before it settles : there were no crusades.
My father died a draughtsman, drawing plans
In an airy well-lit office above the ground
Beneath which his usurpers, other kings,
Reigned by the fallen helmet he resigned
Which I inherit as a concrete husk.
I hand it back to gather dust on the shelf.

THE TIN

Its odd inscription caught my eye
Beside the scales : those words ' cream toffees
In dented gilt across bashed silver
Drove me to lift the lid and look

At what I knew would still be there :
That hammer with a grimed oak handle,
That broken hack-saw, that rusted file,
That *Woolworth's* chisel bent in the middle,

That wriggle of nails, nuts, bolts and screws.
I tipped them out. The tin looked bare
On the swabbed floor; and I felt moved
With sudden grief for the bright void

My face hung in. I felt as if
The tin's caved sides were drained of breath :
As if there were some vacuum
Inside its walls, inside my skin,

That ached to be fulfilled with care
And swell with hope. But those bent sides
Accused my cold reflected eyes
Of what they knew I'd not yet done

And never would. In awkward rage
I flung the tools back in their place
And closed the lid, and shut my mind,
On guilt I couldn't put in words.

A DEATH IN THE NORTH

The fire leaps in the living-room. I poke
Its dying flames. Tar-blackened trucks with coal
Cluttle past the back room window clagged with soot.
Wheels block the snow-bound farm with mottled cows.

Black milk, white anthracite — where two bloods ran
From pit and furrow — mark their mingling lines :
Hers' with blue eyes cold-blow-lamped by the wind
In cheeks filed red from forking swedes in hail;

His with that swamp-rat face from hacking slate
And shoulders hunched from years in pinching seams.
In front the Roman road runs straight as iron
Between the North Sea and the Norsemen's graves

A measured mile. There winged heels flayed the pitch
From bevelled stones where centuries raked the picts
Across that rambling dyke like sheaves of hay.
Those pickaxe noses, that sea-eagle's beak,

Ravage the vision with a dwindling rage.
I see one's tears, another's tightening lips
At that hook-face held rigid for its course
In slow triumph along the bowing road

Towards its final blaze beyond the pits.
Far off above the farm I count the crows.
At the front gate I hear a car's doors close.
I wave away that polished fleet of Rolls

To coast the Roman road : this rigid man
Whose brows I touch — bare flesh like marzipan
Sealed up in golden wrapping — stretched in state
Like a stone flag to keep the cars in line

South from the mining village to the sea.
A bleak wind from the pit-wheels chills the room.
In the black grate his boots are still burning,
Melting leather mingling with white ash.

ST. ANDREW'S

Here in my tight suit, Sunday after Sunday,
I'd shiver in the draughty oblong hall.
(The fire-bomb-gutted church was never used
Except by children or for some church play
That needed ruins.) Here my pimpled skin

Wrinkled in prayer when I propped my head
On my poised fingers : forms of words worn thin
Helped me to remember what should be said.
I'd bend beside my mother, gangling, tall.
I prayed for faith, but felt that God refused.

Let me look back. I'm there in my rough chair,
Bare legs on sharp straw, sucking buttermint
Slipped in my fidgeting hands by fur-gloved hands.
I'm wondering when the intercession-prayer
Will end. More prayers, intimations, hymns

Flounce leisurely on. I watch bulged offering-bags
Shuttle between deacons. Touched coins chink. Stiff limbs
Ease. The soft mouths, whose belly-velvet sags,
Gape for warmed silver, trickling out by dint
Of pressed appeals for ' our missions in far lands '.

The lesson booms out. James McClusky's black
Bony razor-headed bust above the bible
Strops his Highland vowels. Quick Scottish wives
Nudge their slumped husbands. Folded arms, feet slack
On loud planks correct themselves. The Book

Quietly shuts, gold leaves flutter. Towards
The back of the hall the text from Habbakuk
Re-echoes. The draped lectern's tasselled cords
Jerk to swung robes. The minister turns : the table
Quakes to beat fists condemning our distracted lives.

Let me look forward. As I grate on boards
I bump the lion-mouthed mahogany throne
He'd hunch in. It's ground by lecturers now. Dead flowers
Droop on the flat piano from which the Lord's
Thundering praises were wrung. I cough and choke

In dust (it's little played now) and stoop through
To the new church : too elegant in oak
For my taste. I advance to our old pew
Through pipe-warmed air. I sit down, scrape fresh stone
With dragging nailed heels. Here, while quarter-hours

Flake from the tower, I stop. My child's belief
(I now believe) was a Scots exile's; gone
With loosened roots. When the sick wish returns
For the lost country, the dream-Scotland grief
Was noble in, I clutch at *things*, plain things

I've lifted to symbols : compasses, a brooch,
Photographs, draughtsman's T-squares, opal rings.
My faith's planted where prayers can't encroach.
I've grown past God-roots. Why, then, back there on
That warm pew do they prick me? Something turns

Time back. It's Easter Day. I see moved plates
Of diced white bread, starched linen someone clears.
The plates clink closer. Furtively, I choose
Christ's body and blood. The hushed young elder waits,
Then catfoots on. And now I'm swallowing wine

From a glass thimble, rolling the lifeless bread
On my living tongue. I'm keyed for some sure sign
Of something miraculous. Eyes blink; my head
Lifts; and I stare at grown men shedding tears
And my own gooseflesh knees, blue with a bruise.

REMEMBERING GREYSTONES

What did I learn at Greystones, my first school?
Something from clay. I don't mean garden clay
My father sliced like fudge-lumps, broken fudge-lumps,
With a steel spade's-edge. I mean clay for playing with,
Squelching-wet, white stuff : clay mashed flat like dough
On sweating palms; dried hard in brittle spindles
Between slow fingers; caked on backs of hands
Plunged wrist-deep into whitewash in grey clay-bins
Jammed in an art-room's corner to cludge it out.
Clay taught me filth. And what did tar teach me,
Stuck to my shoes' greyed lozenge-patterned rubbers
On the baked asphalt of our melting playground?
Tar taught what fire does. Before war broke out
I'd seen a trapped boy terrified by fire
Forced by six others in a smoke-filled cellar
And kept there coughing, choked with swirling ash;
And another crouching with his tight knees browned
With diarrhoea, blubbing behind the backs
At being nicknamed ' stinker '.
My uncle died floundering through Belgian sludge
In the first World War : my father died in fire
Charred in a Sheffield blitz. Through filth and smoke
Forgotten links with those blood-ridden soldiers
Educate my will. In clay and tar
Two wars collide : fouled bodies from my childhood,
War as the art-room clay, as playground tar,
Sharpens to that boy choking, that boy jeered at :
Tears, diarrhoea : what being burned, being dirty means :
That's what I learned at Greystones, my first school.

THE WASPS' NEST

All day to the loose tile behind the parapet
The droning bombers fled : in the wet gutter
Belly-upwards the dead were lying, numbed
By October cold. And now the bloat queen,
Sick-orange, with wings draped, and feelers trailing,
Like Helen combing her hair, posed on the ledge
Twenty feet above the traffic. I watched, just a foot
From her eyes, very glad of the hard glass parting
My pressed human nose from her angry sting
And her heavy power to warm the cold future
Sunk in unfertilised eggs. And I thought : if I reached
And inched this window open, and cut her in half
With my unclasped pen-knife, I could exterminate
An unborn generation. All next summer,
If she survives, the stepped roof will swarm
With a jam of striped fighters. Therefore, this winter
In burning sulphur in their dug-out hangars
All the bred wasps must die. Unless I kill her.
So I balanced assassination with genocide
As the queen walked on the ledge, a foot from my eyes
In the last sun of the year, the responsible man
With a cold nose, who knew that he must kill,
Coming to no sure conclusion, nor anxious to come.

THE BIRD

When I got home
Last night I found
A bird the cat
Had brought into the house
On the kitchen floor.

It wasn't dead.
It looked as if
It was, at first.
There were some feathers lying
Against the wall :

The bird itself
With its wings folded
Lay and stared.
It didn't move.
I picked it up :

Quivering like a clockwork
Toy in my hand
I carried it out
Into the yard
And put it down

In a slice of light
From the door. I lifted
A long broom
By the handle near to
The head and struck

The bird four times.
The fourth time it
Didn't move.
Blood, in a stringy
Trickle, blotched

48

The white concrete.
I edged the remains
Up with a red
Plastic shovel.
Lifting it through

The house to the *yard*
I tipped it out
In the dust-bin along with
Snakes of fluff
And empty soup-tins.

When I emptied the tea-leaves
This morning I saw
The bird I killed
Leaning its head
On a broken egg-shell.

THE KNIVES

I own four knives that were made for killing. They decorate
    my house. In romantic moods
I picture myself accosting a burglar with one of them. First, a
    Victorian bayonet. This
One took a hell of a lot of guts to handle, I'll bet. It's a heavy
    thing. You can wrench

It in and out of its sheath, but it calls for a certain amount of
    sweat. I've crossed the two
I think of next like swords on my dining-room mantelpiece.
    First, a diminutive fruit-knife, marked
' Enthumion ', Greek for ' a gift ', for the classical tourist : a
    neat little scissor for slitting

An adam's apple. Some kind of juice has rusted the crescent
    steel. It sticks when it slides
From its wooden sheath. And second, my Scottish dirk. It's
    encased in a frayed-cardboard, Cameron-
Tartan holder. I clean its hilt's chased silver once in about six
    months. The dirt's

Ingrained like ash in the curling crevices. The blade has a
    diamond section. It's sharpened
On both sides like an axe. Given a cool head and a steady
    hand you could use
It for peeling potatoes. I don't. The last one's a lightweight
    ivory ' Chinese ' throwing-knife. The tip's

Broken off. And there's dried blood on the blunt edge and the
    words ' Meet Me at Maules '
In copper-plate. There are thirty-eight uneven slots notched in
    the hilt. All men
It's killed, I'd like to think. I wonder why I preserve these four
    not very important knives

I never use or clean. To give them space for decay in a decent
  slowness? In guilt
For a cushioned, inhibited life? I avoid their implications :
  they decorate my house
Through which I walk in the warmth of my five electric fires
  secure from the need to kill.

IMPRESSIONS ON WEARING NEW SPECTACLES

Blinking with cold (the old horn frames were bigger), I
    stepped from the warm shop
Into the fog. I felt slightly off-balance, as if I'd been
    drinking.
Did I look handsome, I wondered? I glanced into windows.
    Not really.
People I knew, like my friends at work, offered ' New
    spectacles, George, eh? '
Just from politeness. I think I was glad : but a little put
    out, too.

How do I feel now? I think of an image : a Georgian house
    when
Casements are changed for sash-windows : more elegant, yes;
    but uneasy.
Things look precise with the spectacles on; with them off, the
    world blurs
Just as it used to. The difference is that I now feel them
    pinch me
Perched on my nose : like a pair of tight-screwed unavoidable
    pincers

Nipping a sort of *spread* face (a complacent look) into a
    peaked look.
Framed in the mirror I face my drawn features with unspoken
    questions :
Am I at ease in these wide-open windows? or does their cold
    glitter
Catch me off guard? Am I faced with a new personality come
    to
Twist or constrict my intentions, envelop me? Well, now, how
    can my

View of this white room be changed when the frames, not the
 lenses, are altered?
Pictures, not frames, are what matter : the lenses are
 certainly new ones,
Ground in a different shape, but the vision they give me is
 unchanged :
Bath, wash-basin, the ' Standard ', and wallpaper fish that
 look blistered.
Yes, this is true. It is I who am changed. But the new frame
 has changed me.

Since the new lenses are smaller, these two twelve-carat-gold
 circles
Narrow the field of my vision : the door, my blown-up duck
 escape as
Vagueness at edges, not objects I know and can handle. The
 room seems
Clear at the centre in logical patterns, but queer at the corners.
This is the reason I feel so uneasy : as if I were squinting

Past my old framework of concepts : had fallen down my
 staircase and stumbled
Suddenly into a strange room not known to be there : had
 watched hinges
Creak back, like casements in tortuous dungeons, on sinister
 vistas :
Insects in watches, hanged women through keyholes, torn flesh
 propped on crutches.
Yes, I've looked into the corners. I know them : that's why
 I look forward.

III

THE ABSENTEES

When Egil Skallagrimsson
Choked Grim's thralls to death at the
Age of eighty though quite blind
The astonished ravens by
The bog were certainly not

You and I. We should hardly
Have stood the spectacle. And
At Bosworth Field when Richard
The Third fell in the thickest
Press of his enemies those

Vultures hovering in the
Black sky were some other glum
Couple. We had better things
To do. Did Gabriele
D'Annunzio observe a

Brace of eagles change into
Pigeons above the fateful
Piave? Those mutable
Birds were perhaps Paola
And Francesca, not you and

I. We were too busy in
Other spheres. Carina, why
Do you worry that we shall
Not be there when the first ape
Steps onto the moon in a

Grey silk hat? I remember
Nothing about the nineteen
Twenties except that I must
Have wet my nappy. The sun
Turns. And your lips invite me.

'THE SPIDER'S NEST'

Was clenched on a fly's carcase like a golden
Fist which exploded into an abacus
Of excited beads at the prick of my quill '

Is one verse. ' This morning I arranged about
A hundred things with legs on invisible
Wires to dance attendance ' is another. To

Be crippled and have such tensed will subdued by
A feather pleases. On a wheeled bed or an
Orbed web life rakes old sores over with my (or

Some other) tough hand. The feather of death in
One's bowels tickles the triumph out of such
Teasing of puissance. Day after day to lie

Here watching the sun skate in the sky, wanting
Death but unable to move except enough
To kill wasps with a book or annoy spiders,

Is something. After all, success in drowning
Ants in vermouth requires only time and I
Collect it like dust. Snakes come. Visitors with

French sonnets. Minestrone for supper. Floods
In May. If Stock insists on a third verse I
Suggest ' a few hesitated between the

Abrupt brink of air and the known centre of
A gauze mesh where their inherited fly lay
Spread out to be eaten ' but I'm not keen on

A fourth verse. To leave great themes unfinished is
Perhaps the most satisfying exercise
Of power. Describing their look of being

The armour of a god left hanging over-
night in a skein of frost can be decently
Left to Vernon. Sleep comes. And with it my snails.

                    Florence, 1885, *Eugene Lee-Hamilton.*

COURT GOSSIP

Despite the College of Physicians
Who claim much can be done, I believe
That a decent prudence would make plans
    For the end of the affair.

They prescribe books : a house in Leyden :
A boy to stoke the furnace. Without
Fail it will all help. In the end, though,
    We shall have to wind things up

With black-edged cards. The old gentleman
Is deranged. For the composition
Of teasing minutes prolonged flogging
    With a quaint thong. Pad sofas

To accommodate that versatile
Negress. Egyptian massage. Full aid
For the nerves. But at what cost ! The
    Exchequer shakes. One shies at

Roman orgies. A dish of truffles :
Coan wine : the ineptitude of
Slave-women. It tots up. The flesh is
    Heir to a mort of torments

But not this. Bustles, hair-splittings — where
Does one draw the line between resigned
Acceptance and a mean carping? Spare
    The rod and spoil the child. I

Anticipate the kiss of Lesbos,
The ' shall we row, darling ', the obscene
Albums. Where is His Royal Highness
    To rove next? A back-scratcher?

Wading with lung-fishes? Assume that
One hires this belly-organ. A sip
Of benedictine, a whiff — and, pish!
   To your leopard-skins, your oiled

Fig silks. I admire the Comtessa's
Alive sense of values. To be suave
In full ruin demands refinement.
   A black banquet is rumoured

For the death of ' a close friend ' : claret :
A burnt chop : Puerto Ricans in tight
Velvet : a scent of burnt wax. Assured
   Boredom for three footmen with

Primed snuffers. Weeping Pierrots. The tears
Running on black net. We inherit
The ash and olive-stones. In a jar
   Of iced honey a ju-jube.

So it ends. The magnificent fails,
Troughed in finger-bowls. The inspired,
Wistful, Athenian faultlessness
   Of Ludwig! And this lecher!

MILDRED

Mildred, our batty cousin, 's been staying with us
Over the weekend. I'm worn out. On Friday
When Mummy and Daddy went to fetch her she wouldn't
Walk downstairs. Mummy said ' Come on, Mildred,
Let's pretend we're bride and groom (shall we?)
And Daddy can be the bridesmaid.' It's always games
To make her do things, childish silly games
I'm sick to death of. She won't do anything
Without persuading. Do you know that twice
When the doctor made an appointment she was out?
Or she wouldn't see him. He'd gone specially
As a favour to us, too. Is she absent-minded
Or just contrary? Well, we don't know which
So we're keeping her locked up at home till she's seen
The psychiatrist on Thursday. Then she'll go home
Or into a home. Her body's cracking up,
Hospital might be better. She's had two strokes.
She's fifty-eight, but she moves as if she was ninety.
And she talks in this infuriating voice
You can't make head or tail of half the time
It's so slurred and slow. Then she's got kidney trouble
So you can imagine the state her flat's in.
No char would stay. And she's so bloody selfish
She'll fly off the handle at the least complaint
Or interference. ' Why can't I — come down
To the drawing- — room and meet — people? ' This morning
She wouldn't dress. Mummy had to put on
All her clothes : every single stitch.
And there's her money. The lawyer said for weeks
She's been drawing twenty pounds out every day
And then spending it. She bought a bubble car.
She bought this beautiful blue starred lino.
She buys Yogurt. We found twenty bottles
Of Yogurt piled up under her bed : all empty.
And about fifteen more unopened, half in
Half out of the fridge. All going bad, some stinking.
She'll spend a pound on lunch. At Coronelli's

This restaurant she goes to she leaves a pound on the table
And just walks out. I don't know what she's doing.
She'll sit there in the dining-room after dinner
Staring ahead of her into empty space
Without looking at anything or moving.
Perhaps she thinks she's back in the theatre.
Theatres are what she's crazy about. Her husband
Victor was manager of *The Globe*. She goes
Four times a week to the pictures, sits in the front row
Wearing her best clothes, claps when the film's over.
We don't want to interfere : but the neighbours
Just take advantage. As things are she can't
Live on her own, though. And you couldn't have anyone
Living in : she takes such violent
Dislikes to people. She had this Italian woman
Marcellina, once. One day she actually
Threw her out : bundled her out of the door
With all her bags. She was the only one
Who was doing Mildred good. She made her work,
Help clean the place up. Ugh ! I pity Granny
Having to sleep in her bed again. She's worse
Than Hank. I hope to God they find some grounds
For doing something definite on Thursday.
If we don't get her certified I'll go mad.

THE VIKING

He doesn't even have strength left to wind his watch
When he wakes up. I can shake sleep out of my body
Like the drops of a shower. I lick his foot
With my rasping tongue, pretending to wash him.

Aw, he says, weakly, rubbing my ear.
He tastes of nothing to me. I can wash and drink
With the same organ, as he can perhaps fornicate
And make water, without comparisons. He needs wool
     blankets

To warm his hollow torso. Even in winter
I curl in the wind and sleep strongly without aids.
I look with a green eye on all copulations,
Doctored by his white vet : but I can be swift

And kill birds on the branch of the mock-orange tree
With a wild leap. Can he? I am alive
Risen from the salt brine and the long barrows
Coiled in a cat's springs. He hasn't even died.

AFTERLIFE

I

I can see in the dark but my eyes
      look much too big
in the soup-tins. I am always
      amazed to see myself.

II

In my wire bowl I can scarcely
      arrange my tail
without bringing a pound of strawberry
      jam on my back. I am too athletic.

III

It helps to be decently tricked out
      with a pair of hands
you could hide in a watch-
      case, of course. I have to spend

so much time eating
to keep warm.

IV

Having gnawed through their Japanese house
      I no longer investigate
rice crispies for signs
      of tops. I am all saliva.

V

The eccentric pleasures of arching at high
      speeds over quite
unbelievably large tracts
      of space are palling.

As are the delights
of messy activities amid flour.

VI

I have not yet approached the arctic
    regions of my world flowing
with milk and honey. Why risk
    such excoriating cold

for wrapped meat?

VII

I could live on the shelves for
    years without touching the ground.
There might be enough cauliflower
    for the rest of my life.

SCISSOR-MAN

I am dangerous
    in a crisis
with sharp legs and a screw

    in my genitals. I slice
bacon-rind for a living. At nights I
    lie dried

under the draining-board, dreaming
    of Nutcrackers
and the Carrot-grater. If I should

    catch him rubbing
those tin nipples of hers
    in the bread-bin

(God rust his pivot!) so much for
    secrecy. I'd have his
washer off. And

    then what? It scarcely pays
to be ' Made In Hamburg '. Even
    our little salt-spoon

can sound snooty
    with an E.P.N.S. under
his armpit. Even the pie-server

    who needs re-dipping. In sixteen
stainless years dividing
    chippolata-links I

am still denied
    a place in the sink unit. And
you can imagine

what pairing-off is possible
with a wriggle of cork-screws
in an open knife-box. So I

keep my legs
crossed. I never cut up
rough. I lie with care

in a world where a squint leg
could be fatal. I sleep like a weapon
with a yen for a pierced ear.

A TRUE STORY

When the British Association
For the Advancement of Science held
Its Annual Meeting one year in
    East Anglia no-one could

Think what to feed them on. It appeared
From previous experience in
County Durham that members consumed
    An enormous quantity

Of sandwiches. How were the hundreds
Of visiting scientists to be
Fed? The problem was finally solved
    By the inspiration of

A Norfolk poacher who suggested
At a public meeting in the Town
Hall at Norwich the employment of
    Their local pest the Coypu

Rat. He claimed that between two layers
Of freshly cut bread a thick slice of
Coypu tasted quite delicious. And
    It proved so. At any rate

The sandwiches were bought and eaten
In extraordinarily large
Numbers. The plain bread seemed to set off
    The unusual taste of

The dead rodent. Indeed a group of
Younger men from the Biology
Section dissected the furry beasts
    With a view to assessing

Just why. Altogether it was ' a
Great success for the quality of
Willingness to experiment ' as
    ' The Countryman ' aptly said.

A CHILD'S GARDEN

Who was here. Before his cat
Washed and rose. Without his shoes
Who inched outside while someone's hat
Made a noise. Light feet helped. Who's.

Whose are these eggs? Ladybird's.
Hard like crumbs of sleep. She flies
Off to help who find some words
For sounds and things. Who's two puffed eyes

Tug at flowers now for bees
Tucked away. Some try to hide
In pouting fox-gloves' jugs. Who sees
Their fat bear's thighs, though, wedged inside

Scouring honey. Look! Rare stones
In lupin leaves. Who's flapping gown
Shakes them all out. Ow! Who's bones
Aren't awake, make who fall down

Biting earth. Who hears a sound.
Whose are these wet softish hairs
Brushing someone's mouth? Can bound
As quick as you. Whoosh! Peter scares

A thin bird. Zip! Squawk! Its beak
Almost nipped who's fattest worm
Head and tail. Who hears him squeak
Through the grass : who sees him squirm

Down a hole. Who wants to kiss
His frightened worm. Who's coolish knees
Push him up to clematis
He thinks it's called. It makes him sneeze.

Gooseflesh comes. Who's bare toes rake
Up oily slugs. Who wants to hop,
Skip. Who's flopping tassels make
Ants run. Who hears his crispies pop.

HOUSE FOR A CHILD

In a corkscrew house you start at the bottom :
You have to : and work up : it might
    Be a world, or a zoo.

Fish freeze on the blotched walls
In the steamy bathroom. I wash my knees
    With a soap poodle who

Smells clean. My thirsty elephant
Floats at my ear : I scrub my feet
    With a bristly pig.

I wrap my crumpled skin in my gown
With wiry tassels and sip juice.
    From a stool in the kitchen

The Peter plunges. He brushes my calves
With his flat sides : his tail shapes
    Ideas he has

In the air. He tortures birds when he can :
Curls in the Beanstalk : shines at night
    Like green slides

In the black garden. I tiptoe in slippers
With loud soles. I trip by the dining-room,
    Kneel and crunch

On crumbs the copper tortoise is crumbling.
I bang on his head : his back clangs up
    And I spit in him.

I nod on my heels to a spider : a quick-stepping
Elderly beetle six-foots himself over
    The blue fur

Of the close floor. I spiral up
Like a fly in a draught. From a cupboard under
        The groaning stairs

The crates creak. I bounce to the drawing-room's
Block of warmth. In a fog of heat
        I tickle the rug

With cool toes. It sheds hair
On mossy suits : laps cream paint
        With a rope tongue.

I light the shelves. The pot pigs blink.
One has a pimply back : he stares :
        If I shook him up,

Now I stare at him, I could hear him juggle
A pea in his throat. In the hall the Kodiak
        Bear by the stove

Stretches and snores. I creep on my tummy
To lie on his back : his coat's warm :
        They thwack his hide

With a hard brush to make him clean.
Good-night, Kodiak bear, sleep tight,
        I roar in his ear as

I flea him of crumbs. I shed the lights
And lock the doors. Now I jump to the bedroom
        To see my owl

Who makes me laugh : I kiss my bear
With his bashed face who keeps me safe
        And who gave his squeak

To a tiny rhino : I kick my slippers
Under the bed. I snuggle down
    Beside my pig.

When you get to the top, you have to stop
In a twiny house : unless you're a worm :
    And go to sleep.

You have to stop : unless you're a worm,
Or a bird : and say good-night : good-night :
    Good-night, world.

BEDTIME STORY

Long long ago when the world was a wild place
Planted with bushes and peopled by apes, our
Mission Brigade was at work in the jungle.
    Hard by the Congo

Once, when a foraging detail was active
Scouting for green-fly, it came on a grey man, the
Last living man, in the branch of a baobab
    Stalking a monkey.

Earlier men had disposed of, for pleasure,
Creatures whose names we scarcely remember —
Zebra, rhinoceros, elephants, wart-hog,
    Lion, rats, deer. But

After the wars had extinguished the cities
Only the wild ones were left, half-naked
Near the Equator : and here was the last one,
    Starved for a monkey.

By then the Mission Brigade had encountered
Hundreds of such men : and their procedure,
History tells us, was only to feed them :
    Find them and feed them;

Those were the orders. And this was the last one.
Nobody knew that he was, but he was. Mud
Caked on his flat grey flanks. He was crouched, half-
    armed with a shaved spear

Glinting beneath broad leaves. When their jaws cut
Swathes through the bark and he saw fine teeth shine,
Round eyes roll round and forked arms waver
    Huge as the rough trunks

Over his head, he was frightened. Our workers
Marched through the Congo before he was born, but
This was the first time perhaps that he'd seen one.
    Staring in hot still

Silence, he crouched there : then jumped. With a long swing
Down from his branch, he had angled his spear too
Quickly, before they could hold him, and hurled it
    Hard at the soldier

Leading the detail. How could he know Queen's
Orders were only to help him? The soldier
Winced when the tipped spear pricked him. Unsheathing his
    Sting was a reflex.

Later the Queen was informed. There were no more
Men. An impetuous soldier had killed off,
Purely by chance, the penultimate primate.
    When she was certain,

Squadrons of workers were fanned through the Congo
Detailed to bring back the man's picked bones to be
Sealed in the archives in amber. I'm quite sure
    Nobody found them

After the most industrious search, though.
Where had the bones gone? Over the earth, dear,
Ground by the teeth of the termites, blown by the
    Wind, like the dodo's.